My Father

Experiencing God's Love A–Z

An Acrostic Devotional By
Pamela A. Taylor

"Looking for the blessed hope and glorious appearing
of our great God and Savior Jesus Christ, who gave Himself
for us, that He might redeem us from every lawless deed
and purify for Himself His own special people,
zealous for good works."
Titus 2:13-14

With Huge Gratitude...

To my Creator God,
for showing me Himself.

To Shelley & CJ Hitz of Christian Book Academy for modeling
and teaching me that publishing a book is possible.

To Heather Hart, who actually made happen all that seemed too
overwhelming until she agreed to be my Author Assistant.
She made it all come alive for you.

Dedicated...

To my prayer team.
Especially to Mary Ann, my spiritual mother,
and dear friends Jo, Lori, and Emily,
who kept believing when I did not.

And to the best Father, Son, Husband and Friend
that anyone could ever hope for – God, the Father,
the Lord Jesus Christ, and the Holy Spirit.

Thank You.

Table of Contents

Introduction

Sometimes it's hard to center down and pray. In those times, I've found the discipline of following the structure of the alphabet helps me keep focused. It helps me clear my mind of other things so I can rest in Him who *is* my rest.

My hope is that *My Father: Experiencing God's Love A-Z* acrostic devotional will get you started seeing God with fresh eyes. Helping you feel more confident in your relationship with Jesus in thought and prayer.

Perhaps you will find this A-Z approach to be a fun activity with your kids. Maybe on a road trip or walking out in nature. Finding additional words to describe *your* Father God. The possibilities are endless. I'd love to hear from you about how A-Z has enriched your relationship with God.

A

My Father, Thank You That You Are **Always There.**

Your Word says…

"…I am with you always, even to the end of the age."
Matthew 28:20b

No matter what happens; no matter how far I stray;
no matter how tired I am, or how ill I feel;
no matter how angry or lonely I am,
I can run back to the arms of my loving Father,
because You are always there.

Thank You.

Journal Your Prayer

_____

_____

_____

_____

_____

_____

_____

_____

_____

_____

_____

_____

_____

_____

_____

_____

_____

_____

_____

My Father, Thank You That You **Believe In Me**.

Your Word says…

"If you can believe, all things are possible to him who believes."
Mark 9:23

Even if I can't believe in myself; even if others criticize and
discourage me from trying new things; even if it has
never been done before, still, You believe in me.

Thank You.

Journal Your Prayer

_____

_____

_____

_____

_____

_____

_____

_____

_____

_____

_____

_____

_____

_____

_____

_____

_____

C

My Father, Thank You That You **Care About Me**.

Your Word says…

"Give all your worries and cares to God, for he cares about you."
1 Peter 5:7 (NLT)

This world seems so lonely sometimes; everyone is busy just
trying to survive, but I can always count on You,
because You care about me.

Thank You.

Journal Your Prayer

_____

_____

_____

_____

_____

_____

_____

_____

_____

_____

_____

_____

_____

_____

_____

_____

_____

_____

My Father, Thank You That You
Are **Devoted To Me.**

Your Word says…

"God has said, 'I will never leave you or let you be alone.'"
Hebrews 13:5 (NLV)

Even marriage vows are taken lightly these days.
Friends come and go, and relatives forget they are
related to each other, but You are devoted to me.

Thank You.

Journal Your Prayer

_____

_____

_____

_____

_____

_____

_____

_____

_____

_____

_____

_____

_____

_____

_____

_____

_____

My Father, Thank You That You Are **Everywhere**.

Your Word says…

"The eyes of the Lord are everywhere,
keeping watch on the wicked and the good."
Proverbs 15:3 (NIV)

In my home, in my work, in my play and in my sleep;
in the flowers and in the rain; in happy people and in sad ones.
You are everywhere in my world.

Thank You.

Journal Your Prayer

_____

_____

_____

_____

_____

_____

_____

_____

_____

_____

_____

_____

_____

_____

_____

_____

_____

My Father, Thank You That You
Are **My Faithful Father.**

Your Word says…

"Lord, you are our father!
You are the one who has always saved us!"
Isaiah 63:16b (ESV)

Fathers are busy. They have work to do.
They travel and sometimes forget they have families.
But, I can look to You to be my Forever Faithful Father.

You are never busy, and You never forget.

Thank You.

Journal Your Prayer

_____

_____

_____

_____

_____

_____

_____

_____

_____

_____

_____

_____

_____

_____

_____

_____

My Father, Thank You That You Are **Generous** To Me.

Your Word says…

"So I say to you: Ask and it will be given to you; seek and you
will find; knock and the door will be opened to you."
Luke 11:9 (NIV)

"If you abide in Me, and My words abide in you, you will ask
what you desire, and it shall be done for you."
John 15:7

You own the cattle on a thousand hills and love giving me
my heart's desires. You tell me to ask and seek and I will
find what I need in You. You are generous to me.

Thank You.

Journal Your Prayer

_____

_____

_____

_____

_____

_____

_____

_____

_____

_____

_____

_____

_____

_____

_____

_____

_____

_____

H

My Father, Thank You That You Are My **Hope-Giver.**

Your Word says…

"For I know the plans I have for you," declares the Lord,
"plans to prosper you and not to harm you,
plans to give you hope and a future."
Jeremiah 29:11 (NIV)

In a world that screams in hopelessness, You show the way.
You are the way to believe again. You are my hope-giver.

Thank You.

Journal Your Prayer

_____

_____

_____

_____

_____

_____

_____

_____

_____

_____

_____

_____

_____

_____

_____

_____

_____

_____

_____

I

My Father, Thank You That You Are **Interested In Me.**

Your Word says…

"Then you will call upon Me and go and pray to Me,
and I will listen to you."
Jeremiah 29:12

When it seems no one cares about my latest success or that I am
sad or that I lost my way, I can stop wherever I am and talk to
You, because You are interested in me.

Thank You.

Journal Your Prayer

_____

_____

_____

_____

_____

_____

_____

_____

_____

_____

_____

_____

_____

_____

_____

_____

_____

_____

J

My Father, Thank You That You Are My **Joy-Giver**.

Your Word says…

"You turned my wailing into dancing;
you removed my sackcloth and clothed me with joy."
Psalm 30:11 (NIV)

Whether it is a sad movie, or my best friend just moved away,
or I am suddenly an orphan because my last parent died,
You fill my emptiness and prove to me that in my sorrow,
You are my joy-giver.

Thank You.

Journal Your Prayer

_____

_____

_____

_____

_____

_____

_____

_____

_____

_____

_____

_____

_____

_____

_____

_____

_____

_____

K

My Father, Thank You That You Are **Kind** To Me.

Your Word says…

"Show your amazing kindness and rescue those who depend on you. Use your great power and protect them from their enemies."
Psalm 17:7 (ERV)

Others may ignore or make fun of me, or push in front of me
in the check-out line, but I can count on the fact that
no matter what -You will be kind to me.

Thank You.

Journal Your Prayer

_____

_____

_____

_____

_____

_____

_____

_____

_____

_____

_____

_____

_____

_____

_____

_____

_____

_____

_____

L

My Father, Thank You That You Are **Longsuffering**.

Your Word says…

"…the longsuffering of our Lord is salvation; even as our beloved brother Paul also according to the wisdom given unto him hath written unto you."
2 Peter 3:15 (KJV)

"Because of the Lord's faithful love we do not perish, for His mercies never end. They are new every morning; great is Your faithfulness!"
Lamentations 3:22-23 (HCSB)

You are forgiving, patient, and uncomplaining in all things that we do together, my Father. I am glad to know that You are so longsuffering with me.

Thank You.

Journal Your Prayer

_____

_____

_____

_____

_____

_____

_____

_____

_____

_____

_____

_____

_____

_____

_____

_____

_____

_____

M

My Father, Thank You That You Are **Mindful of Me**.

Your Word says…

"You've kept track of all my wandering and my weeping. You've stored my many tears in your bottle—not one will be lost. For they are all recorded in your book of remembrance."
Psalm 56:8 (TPT)

Oh, my precious Father, You are so aware of my pain, disappointments, hurts, and tears. I am never away from Your watchful eye. You are forever mindful of me.

Thank You.

Journal Your Prayer

_____

_____

_____

_____

_____

_____

_____

_____

_____

_____

_____

_____

_____

_____

_____

_____

_____

My Father, Thank You That You Are **Never Too Busy** For Me.

Your Word says…

"I know that when l call for help, my enemies will turn and run. I know that because God is with me!"
Psalm 56:9 (ERV)

Though others may grow weary, it doesn't matter what time of the day or night that I cry out to You Father, You are never hurried, never too busy.

Thank You.

Journal Your Prayer

_____

_____

_____

_____

_____

_____

_____

_____

_____

_____

_____

_____

_____

_____

_____

_____

_____

_____

My Father, Thank You That You Are **Open-Armed**.

Your Word says…

"This I declare about the Lord: He alone is my refuge, my place
of safety; he is my God, and I trust him"
Psalm 91:2 (NLT)

You are wherever I am. You are open-armed, and always
a place of comfort and refuge. Your arms are
never closed to me – I am Your child.

Thank You.

Journal Your Prayer

_____

_____

_____

_____

_____

_____

_____

_____

_____

_____

_____

_____

_____

_____

_____

_____

My Father, Thank You That You Are **My Provider**.

Your Word says…

"The Lord is my rock, and my fortress, and my deliverer;
my God, my strength, in whom I will trust; my buckler,
and the horn of my salvation, and my high tower."
Psalm 18:2 (KJV)

Whatever I need, dear Father, You are it – whether it be physical,
emotional, mental, spiritual, or financial. You are my provider.

Thank You.

Journal Your Prayer

_____

_____

_____

_____

_____

_____

_____

_____

_____

_____

_____

_____

_____

_____

_____

_____

Q

My Father, Thank You That You Are **Quiet-Spoken**.

Your Word says…

"the Lord passed by, and a great and strong wind tore into the
mountains and broke the rocks in pieces before the Lord,
but the Lord was not in the wind; and after the wind an
earthquake, but the Lord was not in the earthquake; and
after the earthquake a fire, but the Lord was not in
the fire; and after the fire a still small voice."
1 Kings 19:11b-12

In this noisy world, where so many people are raising their voices
in order to be heard, You lower Yours. You are quiet-spoken.

Thank You.

Journal Your Prayer

_____

_____

_____

_____

_____

_____

_____

_____

_____

_____

_____

_____

_____

_____

_____

_____

_____

_____

My Father, Thank You That You
Are **Right Alongside Me.**

Your Word says…

"He leads me beside the still waters. He restores my soul; He leads me in the paths of righteousness For His name's sake."
Psalm 23:2b-3

It is an encouragement to know that I am not alone, Daddy. In every moment and in all the things I do, You are right alongside me, holding my hand.

Thank You.

Journal Your Prayer

_____

_____

_____

_____

_____

_____

_____

_____

_____

_____

_____

_____

_____

_____

_____

_____

_____

_____

S

My Father, Thank You That You Are **Steadily Dependable.**

Your Word says…

"The Lord is the One who will go before you.
He will be with you; He will not leave you or forsake you.
Do not be afraid or discouraged."
Deuteronomy 31:8 (HCSB)

My Father, You are always available, always holding
my armor on, and continually, consistently,
and steadily dependable, in all things.

Thank You.

Journal Your Prayer

T

My Father, Thank You That You Are **Trustworthy.**

Your Word says…

"God is not human, that he should lie, not a human being, that
he should change his mind. Does he speak and then not act?
Does he promise and not fulfill?"
Numbers 23:19 (NIV)

My Father, it is so good to know that I can believe Your Word -
that You do not lie and that You care for Your own.
I am so grateful that You are trustworthy.
Thank You.

Journal Your Prayer

_____

_____

_____

_____

_____

_____

_____

_____

_____

_____

_____

_____

_____

_____

_____

_____

_____

_____

_____

U

My Father, Thank You That You Are **Unwavering**.

Your Word says…

"I have loved you with an everlasting love; therefore, I have
continued to extend faithful love to you."
Jeremiah 31:3b (HCSB)

Others may have a love that is conditional and fragile, but I know
that You are dependable and unwavering with Your love, always
intently pursuing until Your children become Your bride.

Thank You.

Journal Your Prayer

_____

_____

_____

_____

_____

_____

_____

_____

_____

_____

_____

_____

_____

_____

_____

_____

_____

$\mathcal{V}$

My Father, Thank You That You Are the **Victor**.

Your Word says…

"For whatever is born of God overcomes the world. And this is
the victory that has overcome the world—our faith."
1 John 5:8

Satan wanted to keep me from You, my Father, but You are
Victor over Satan. Although he wins a few skirmishes,
You have already won the war.

Thank You.

Journal Your Prayer

W

My Father, Thank You That You
Want Time With Me.

Your Word says…

"The Lord your God in your midst,
The Mighty One, will save;
He will rejoice over you with gladness,
He will quiet you with His love,
He will rejoice over you with singing."
Zephaniah 3:17

Sometimes it is hard to comprehend that You want time with me
– and that I don't have to do anything special to earn Your
attention. That makes me feel very good, my Father.

Thank You.

Journal Your Prayer

_____

_____

_____

_____

_____

_____

_____

_____

_____

_____

_____

_____

_____

_____

_____

_____

_____

_____

My Father, Thank You That You Are **"X"-tatic.**

Your Word says…

> "And you will seek Me and find Me,
> when you search for Me with all your heart."
> Jeremiah 29:13

That is really awesome, my Father – that You are ecstatic
when I seek You and desire to spend time with You. It is hard to
understand why someone as important as You would delight to
spend time with me, and yet it is true!

Thank You.

Journal Your Prayer

_____

_____

_____

_____

_____

_____

_____

_____

_____

_____

_____

_____

_____

_____

_____

_____

_____

_____

Y

My Father, Thank You That You **Yearn For Me.**

Your Word says…

"Or do you think it's without reason the Scripture says that the
Spirit who lives in us yearns jealously?"
James 4:5 (HCSB)

The more I spend time in the Scriptures, reading how You relate
to Your people, the more I see that You do indeed yearn for me,
Your bride, in deep relationship.

Thank You.

Journal Your Prayer

My Father, Thank You That You Are **Zealous**.

Your Word says…

"You will be called the People God Loves, and your land will be
called the Bride of God, because the Lord loves you. And your
land will belong to him as a bride belongs to her husband.
As a young man marries a woman, so your children will
marry your land. As a man rejoices over his new wife,
so your God will rejoice over you."
Isaiah 62:4b-5 (NCV)

Earnest, enthusiastic and eager, You are zealous in Your love for
me, Your bride. You shower me with blessings daily. Make me
ever mindful of You and zealous in my love for You in return.

Thank You.

Journal Your Prayer

_____

_____

_____

_____

_____

_____

_____

_____

_____

_____

_____

_____

_____

_____

_____

_____

_____

_____

Got a Minute?

If this devotional has impacted your life,
please take a moment to let someone know.
Here are a few ways you can show your support:

Write a book review.

Share or mention *My Father* on social media.
Be sure to use the hashtag #MyFatherAcrosticDevo.

Recommend this book to your friends, family,
Bible study sisters, church family, or anyone else
you think might enjoy it as much as you have.

Connect with Pam online by visiting
LoavesandFishesCoaching.com.

About The Author

Pam Taylor is passionately in love with Jesus Christ and delights in walking with Him daily. Her greatest joy has been providing for and raising her two adult children. As a result of being a single, homeschooling mom and former missionary to third world countries, Pam discovered her gifts for teaching, discipling, and writing. She is now a Christian Life Coach and Living Your Strengths Mentor.

You can learn more about Pam and connect with her online at LoavesandFishesCoaching.com

Also Available

From a flock of geese to a dog on a leash, the pages of this winsome little book are filled with things we see around us every day. Pamela A. Taylor takes those everyday items and looks at them through the eyes of a child; making them seem exciting and new while also teaching children how to be grateful for the God who created them. Take a walk with Pamela through the pages of this book and help your little ones see God's hand in the beauty of life.

Daddy Daddy is available wherever books are sold.